FISHI...

1

Other titles by Danny Byrne :-

Danny Gets to Grips with **Football**
Danny Gets to Grips with **Gardening**
Danny Gets to Grips with **Golf**
Danny Gets to Grips with **Horse & Pony Care**
Danny Gets to Grips with the **Motor Car**

Danny
GETS TO GRIPS WITH
FISHING

DC Publishing Paperback

First edition 1996

DC Publishing
11 Bryanston Village
Blandford Forum
Dorset DT11 0PR

Made and printed in Great Britain

For my nephew Darren,
the dedicated fisherman, who has
many tales to tell of the 'one that got away'.
(Almost as many tales as excuses for
arriving home late.)

CONTENTS

FOREWORD

"Having sampled most fishing cartoon books over the years, I have absolutely no hesitation whatsover in strongly recommending this superbly illustrated work from the artistic pen of Danny Byrne.

Not only does it bring back fond memories of my own less illustrious exploits, but never before have I enjoyed such graphic, even technical detail so accurately married to the subject of fishing humour, and I just know the reader will love the drawings, and laugh at the following pages.

Good Fishing!

John Wilson

INTRODUCTION

Take up fishing and you're hooked for life.

Being outside is exhilarating and heightens
all our senses.

Ask a million anglers why fishing is the greatest pastime and you will receive a wide range of differing answers.

You'll never forget the excitement of that
first prize catch.

One attraction must be the mystery
element.....impossible to predict what might
happen next.

Busy stretches of canals and rivers have their
own unexpected excitement.

With new modern tackle, fishing is now
less complicated.

You'll enjoy the thrill of a good fish streaking off
with your bait.

Beware the sudden arc of the rod.

The thrill of the chase is an experience
not to be missed.

You'll come to love and respect
all aspects of outdoor life.

SAFETY FIRST

Try never to go fishing alone!

A firm footing is important to prevent falling in.

Old jetties can provide great fishing platforms.

Beware unforeseen dangers.

Tell others where you are and when
you will be back.

THE FISHING TACKLE

Fishing can be relatively inexpensive.

It's important to feel comfortable
with your new tackle.

Retailers go to great lengths to offer a
good after sales service.

A carryall is advisable
but must be manageable.

It's impossible to know what float you may need.
Be prepared!

Keepnet ...A must to hold all your catch.

A bait-waiter will make feeding simpler.

Rod restheads are essential for those
long tiring days.

A good umbrella will keep you and
your tackle dry.

A disgorger and forceps allow for quick
humane removal of hooks.

Wellington boots are recommended,
but don't go out of your depth!

Keep dry! A decent pair of waders
is a good investment.

To weigh your prize catch, a digital scale is
accurate and easy to read.

A landing net....
for all those happy landings.

Remember insects thrive near water.
Insect repellent is certainly worth having at hand.

FISHING WEATHER

Be prepared for all weather conditions.

Barometers are a good device for telling us of
any change in the climate.

FOLK LORE

Good tips in age old sayings

'Red sky at night, anglers delight.
Arrive early...Give the fish a fright.'

FOLK LORE

Good tips in age old sayings

'Grey mist at dawn..
Fish biting at dusk and early morn.'

FOLK LORE

Good tips in age old sayings

'Rain before seven
Fat fish by eleven.'

FOLK LORE

Good tips in age old sayings

'Wind blowing from the South or West
Bags the biggest and the best.'

All creatures respond to changes in the weather.

When gnats cloud in the early morning
the day will be sunny.

Persistent croaking by one or more crows
indicates rain.

BAIT

Store maggots in a cool place to prevent them turning into flies.

Used sparingly, bread is a cheap source of
buoyant bait.

Many anglers flavour their bread paste
with honey.

Luncheon meat is a favourite for fish.

Earthworms provide a plentiful source of bait.

The redworm is a very lively worm and is
commonly found in compost heaps.

Lobworms are the largest of the worm family and
have excellent fish-drawing qualities.

THE FISHING TRIP

Think positive!
Anticipate the really big catch.

Always think one step ahead.

To catch fish, firstly get to know them.

Crouch or crawl towards open bankside to
prevent frightening the fish.

Try to blend in with the background.

It's important that you are familiar with
a selection of knots.

The overhead cast for long distances.

The underarm cast is effortless and ideal to use
at the end of a hard days fishing.

Casting in the wind causes its own difficulties.

Pole fishing's greatest advantage is being able
to fish where the traditional rod can't reach.

Never hurry, take your time and your catch will
be worth all the trouble you've taken.

THE BITE, STRIKE & LANDING

The Bite.
When your float darts under the water.

Strike immediately. Be firm and positive.

When reeling-in play with the fish, but remain in
complete control.

Be prepared for the fish to suddenly gain a
second wind.

When fish show signs of tiring reach for the
landing net.

FLY FISHING

Fly fishing is a very skilful sport and demands a
great deal of accuracy.

To avoid low hanging branches, the side cast
must be learnt and adopted.

Don't be distracted from learning good technique
from the many flashy fly designs available.

Always look behind you before casting to see if
there are any obstructions which you may snag.

Practise and you'll soon master
the art of fly fishing.

KNOW YOUR FISH

The Rainbow trout
The beautifully formed
trout is an invader
from the U.S.A.

Very nice
smoked

Zander
A particular feature of this fish
is its large eyes.
A master of finding food in
unexpected circumstances.

Barbel
A very exciting sport fish for any angler to attempt to catch as they never give up in a fight.

Dace
You'll need very quick reactions and a rapid strike to catch this small silvery fish.

91

Salmon
King of the fish.
The best known
record-breaking
fish in the world.

Brown trout
This fish lives
in cold rivers
and lakes fed
by cool springs
and melted snow.

Pike

Britain's largest predatory fish.
The angler's catch of a lifetime.
The fish most talked about in the
saying, 'The one that got away'.

Ruffe

Rough scales and
prickly dorsal fins.
This small unfriendly
fish is certainly a
match for most anglers.

Grayling
The elegant grayling is
commonly known as
the lady of the stream

Eel
On maturing, the eel makes its amazing journey
downstream, across the Atlantic, to the Bahamas
to spawn.

Chub
Known as the greedy chub because of its large mouth and voracious appetite

Carp
The crafty carp can tax the ingenuity of even the best anglers.

The best loved fish of all comes battered
with a few chips.